Credit Mastery for HELOC Approval

How to Maximize Your Score, Limits, and Loan Terms

By Joseph G. Correa

Licensed Mortgage Broker, Finibi Mortgage

Copyright & Legal Notice

First Edition, 2026

Table of Contents

Foreword

Most homeowners believe their ability to access home equity is determined by how much their house is worth, how much income they earn, or how long they have owned their home. In reality, the single most powerful factor in whether you get approved for a HELOC, how much you are approved for, and how cheap or expensive that money becomes is your credit profile. Credit is the language lenders use to translate risk into dollars. It is the lens through which every underwriter sees you, no matter how much equity you have or how responsible you feel you are. This book exists because most people never learn how that lens actually works. They are told vague rules like "keep your score high" or "pay your bills on time," but they are never taught how lenders truly analyze risk, how algorithms weigh different data points, or how to intentionally shape their credit profile so it works in their favor instead of against them. If you have ever wondered why one homeowner gets approved for a six-figure HELOC while another is denied or offered terrible terms despite having similar income and equity, the answer lives in this invisible world of credit logic.

Over years of working with homeowners, investors, self-employed borrowers, and families across every credit tier, I have seen how misunderstood credit really is. I have watched people with high incomes and beautiful homes get rejected because their revolving utilization was too high or their profile was too thin. I have also watched people with average incomes and modest homes unlock massive credit lines simply because their credit was engineered correctly. This is not luck. It is not favoritism. It is math. It is risk modeling. It is probability. The system is not designed to reward effort, intelligence, or even honesty. It is designed to reward predictability. Lenders are not trying to decide whether you are a good person. They are trying to determine how likely you are to pay them back based on patterns from millions of borrowers before you. Once you understand that, you stop being emotional about credit and start becoming strategic. That shift alone can change your financial life.

A HELOC is one of the most powerful financial tools available to homeowners, but it is also one of the most sensitive to credit. Unlike a fixed mortgage, which locks in once and stays mostly static, a HELOC behaves more like a living financial instrument. It has a variable rate, a revolving balance, and an ongoing risk assessment. Lenders look at HELOC borrowers more carefully because they know that access to liquid credit increases behavior risk. Someone with $200,000 sitting on a line of credit can do great things with it—or terrible ones. Because of that, the credit standards for HELOCs are often stricter and more nuanced than people realize. This is why someone might qualify easily for a purchase loan but struggle to get a HELOC, even with plenty of equity. This book was written to close that knowledge gap and give you control over how lenders see you.

Credit mastery is not about chasing a number. A 720 score means very different things depending on how it is built. Two people with the same score can have wildly different approval outcomes, interest rates, and credit limits. That is because underwriters and automated systems look far beyond the headline score. They analyze utilization patterns, account age, mix of credit, inquiry timing, payment consistency, and dozens of behavioral signals that most consumers never see. When you understand those signals, you gain the ability to optimize not just your score, but your entire financial footprint. You stop reacting to credit reports and start designing them. You stop hoping for approvals and start engineering them.

This book is not written for people who want to be passive about their finances. It is written for homeowners who want to use their equity as a tool for freedom, security, and growth. Whether your goal is to eliminate debt, fund a business, invest in real estate, or simply have access to low-cost emergency capital, your credit will either be the bridge or the barrier. Most people unknowingly build barriers. They open and close accounts at the wrong time, carry balances that send the wrong risk signals, and apply for loans in ways that sabotage their own profiles. None of this is because they are irresponsible. It is because no one ever explained the rules. This book exists to do exactly that.

You will learn how to position your credit profile specifically for HELOC approval, not just generic lending. You will learn how to manage revolving balances so they increase your limits instead of shrinking them. You will learn how to time applications, optimize utilization, and structure your accounts so lenders view you as stable, predictable, and low risk. You will also learn how to fix common credit mistakes that quietly kill HELOC deals, even for borrowers who look good on paper. These strategies are not theoretical. They are based on real underwriting models, real lender behavior, and real approval data from the front lines of mortgage and home equity lending.

As a licensed mortgage broker working with homeowners every day, I have seen how life-changing a properly structured HELOC can be. I have watched families wipe out high-interest debt, stabilize their cash flow, and finally breathe again. I have seen entrepreneurs fund businesses without giving up equity. I have seen investors buy property, renovate, and scale faster than they ever thought possible. And I have also seen people lose opportunities because their credit was working against them without them realizing it. The difference between those two outcomes is knowledge and strategy. This book is designed to give you both.

Credit is not something to fear. It is something to master. When you do, your home stops being just a place to live and starts becoming a financial engine. The purpose of this book is to help you take control of that engine so it works for you, not the other way around. By the time you finish this foreword, you should already sense that this is not just another book about credit. It is a playbook for unlocking the full financial potential of your home through intelligent, intentional credit design. That is the path to real financial freedom, and it starts here.

Chapter 1

How HELOC Lenders Actually See Your Credit

Most borrowers believe a HELOC lender looks at their credit score and simply decides yes or no based on that number. In reality, that score is only a surface indicator of a much deeper system that measures risk behavior, liquidity management, and long-term financial stability. When a lender evaluates you for a HELOC, they are not asking whether you paid your bills in the past; they are asking whether you will manage access to tens or hundreds of thousands of dollars in the future without becoming financially unstable. The scoring system exists to predict behavior under stress, not reward good intentions. That is why people with high incomes and large homes are often rejected while others with modest means are approved for large lines of credit. The difference is how their credit profile signals risk.

HELOC lenders are especially sensitive to revolving credit behavior. Revolving credit includes credit cards, lines of credit, and any account where you can borrow, repay, and borrow again. Because a HELOC is itself a revolving credit product, lenders look closely at how you manage similar accounts. Someone who maxes out cards, pays the minimum, and cycles debt looks risky even if they never miss a payment. Someone who keeps balances low, pays down strategically, and lets accounts age looks predictable. Predictability is the single most valuable trait in credit underwriting. A lender wants to know not just whether you pay, but whether your financial behavior is stable and repeatable over time.

The three biggest factors that influence HELOC approval are revolving utilization, credit profile depth, and payment consistency. Revolving utilization is the percentage of your available credit that you are using. If you have $50,000 in credit card limits and $25,000 in balances, you are using 50 percent of your available credit. To a HELOC lender, that signals stress, even if you are paying on time. Credit profile depth refers to how many active accounts you have, how long they have been open, and how diverse they are. A thin profile with only a few accounts is less reliable than a thick profile with many well-managed lines. Payment consistency is not just about whether you paid on time, but whether your balances trend downward, stay stable, or grow.

Another factor most borrowers never realize is that lenders do not view debt as bad by default. They view unmanaged debt as dangerous. A borrower with $40,000 in card balances on $200,000 of limits looks much safer than a borrower with $10,000 of balances on $12,000 of limits. The first borrower is using only 20 percent of their capacity while the second is using over 80 percent. Even though the second borrower owes less, they look far riskier because they have almost no remaining credit buffer. HELOC lenders are obsessed with buffers. They want to see that you could absorb financial shocks without spiraling into default.

The way credit bureaus calculate scores also matters. There is not one score. There are dozens of scoring models, and mortgage and HELOC lenders use versions that heavily weight revolving utilization and payment patterns. A borrower might see a 720 score on an app, but the mortgage-grade score used for HELOC underwriting might be 30 to 50 points lower depending on utilization and account structure. This is why people are shocked when their lender tells them they are below the threshold even though their app says they are fine. Understanding this difference is critical because it changes how you prepare before applying.

Finally, HELOC lenders analyze how new credit, inquiries, and account changes have affected you over the last six to twelve months. Rapid new accounts, balance spikes, or missed payments create volatility, and volatility equals risk. The ideal HELOC borrower looks boring on paper. Their balances move slowly. Their accounts are seasoned. Their credit usage is low and consistent. They are not constantly opening and closing accounts. This boring profile is what unlocks high limits, low rates, and smooth approvals. In the rest of this book, you will learn how to intentionally build that profile.

Practical Example

Let's look at two homeowners, Alex and Maria, who both want a $150,000 HELOC. Both own homes worth $500,000 and owe $250,000 on their mortgages, so both have $250,000 in equity. On the surface, they look identical. But their credit profiles tell two very different stories. Alex has five credit cards with a total limit of $40,000 and balances of $32,000. His utilization is $32,000 divided by $40,000, which equals 80 percent. Maria has eight credit cards with a total limit of $120,000 and balances of $18,000. Her utilization is $18,000 divided by $120,000, which equals 15 percent. Even though Maria owes less than Alex, she also has far more unused credit available, which signals stability.

Now look at how a HELOC lender interprets this. Alex has only $8,000 of remaining credit before he is maxed out. That means if an emergency happens, he has almost no buffer. Maria has $102,000 of unused credit. That means even if she experiences financial stress, she has massive flexibility to manage it. To a lender, Maria looks dramatically safer. That difference alone can result in Maria being approved for a $150,000 HELOC at a low rate while Alex might be denied or approved for only $30,000 at a much higher rate.

Next, consider their payment behavior. Alex pays $800 per month on his credit cards, but his balances stay the same because interest keeps them high. Maria pays $600 per month, but her balances go down because she pays more than the interest. Over six months, Alex still owes $32,000. Maria goes from $18,000 to $14,000. Lenders see that Maria's trend is downward while Alex's is flat. That trend signals whether someone is gaining control or slowly losing it.

Now factor in score impact. Alex's high utilization pushes his mortgage-grade score down to 660. Maria's low utilization keeps her score at 735. Many HELOC programs require 700 or higher. Even though both have equity and income, Alex misses the cutoff and Maria qualifies. That difference could mean Alex pays 10 percent interest while Maria pays 7 percent. On a $150,000 HELOC, that is the difference between $15,000 per year in interest and $10,500 per year. Over five years, Maria saves $22,500 simply because her credit profile was structured better.

This example shows why HELOC lending is not about how much you owe, but how you owe it. Maria could borrow $150,000 and still look safe to a lender because her utilization would remain manageable. Alex borrowing that same amount would push him into a danger zone because he already operates at high risk levels. The lender does not guess this. The math makes it obvious.

This is why the goal of credit mastery is not just paying bills but engineering ratios. When you understand how these numbers work, you can change how lenders see you. You are no longer hoping for approval. You are designing it.

Chapter 2

The Credit Score Illusion and What HELOC Lenders Really Use

Most borrowers walk into a HELOC application believing their credit score is a single, universal number that every lender sees. They might open a credit app, see a 720 or a 740, and assume they are perfectly qualified. What they do not realize is that there are dozens of scoring models, and the score shown on consumer apps is almost never the one a HELOC lender uses. Mortgage and home equity lenders rely on older, more conservative models that punish revolving balances, recent credit activity, and thin profiles much more harshly. This is why so many homeowners feel blindsided when a lender tells them their score is too low even though their app says otherwise. The number you see is marketing. The number the lender sees is underwriting.

The most common consumer scores come from VantageScore models, which are designed to be optimistic and forgiving. They are built to keep people engaged with credit monitoring services. HELOC lenders, however, use FICO mortgage-grade scores such as FICO 2, 4, and 5. These models were built to protect lenders from risk, not make borrowers feel good. They weigh revolving utilization far more heavily, penalize new accounts more aggressively, and respond more slowly to recent improvements. A borrower who pays off a credit card today might see their app score jump in a week, but their mortgage score may not fully reflect that change for 30 to 60 days. That delay alone can cause a HELOC application to fail.

Revolving credit is the biggest point of divergence between these models. Consumer scores tolerate balances as long as payments are made. Mortgage scores assume that high balances mean future instability. If your utilization is above 30 percent, your mortgage-grade score is already being suppressed. If it is above 50 percent, the penalty becomes severe. If it is above 70 percent, you are considered high risk regardless of your income or payment history. This is why people who "never miss a payment" still get rejected. They are financially alive, but they are credit-risk dead.

Another hidden factor is how many accounts are reporting balances. You might only owe $10,000, but if that $10,000 is spread across five cards instead of one, the scoring model interprets that as greater dependency on credit. Mortgage scores prefer fewer accounts with balances, even if the total amount owed is the same. This is why strategic balance placement matters. Where the debt lives is just as important as how much it is. HELOC lenders also care about how recently you used credit. A flurry of new inquiries, balance transfers, or new accounts in the last six months signals financial motion. Motion equals risk. Even if those changes were responsible, the model cannot see your intentions. It only sees patterns that historically lead to default. The safest borrower is not the one who is working the hardest, but the one whose profile looks calm and stable over time.

Finally, HELOC lenders look at layered risk. They do not just look at your score in isolation. They combine it with loan-to-value, income type, property type, and cash reserves. A borrower with a 720 score and 80 percent LTV looks far riskier than a borrower with a 700 score and 50 percent LTV. Credit interacts with every other variable. That is why mastering credit is not about chasing perfection, but about optimizing how all these elements work together to make you look safe to a lender.

Practical Example

Consider two borrowers, Jason and Linda. Jason checks his credit app and sees a 745 score. Linda sees a 715. Jason assumes he is the stronger borrower. But when they apply for HELOCs, Jason's mortgage-grade score comes back at 685, while Linda's comes back at 710. The reason is utilization and account structure. Jason has $25,000 in card limits and $15,000 in balances, which is 60 percent utilization. Linda has $80,000 in limits and $12,000 in balances, which is 15 percent utilization. Even though Jason's app score is higher, his mortgage score is lower because high utilization is heavily punished in HELOC underwriting.

Now look at the interest rate impact. Jason qualifies for a HELOC at 9.5 percent because his mortgage score is below 700. Linda qualifies at 7.5 percent. Both borrow $100,000. Jason pays $9,500 per year in interest. Linda pays $7,500. Over five years, Jason pays $47,500 while Linda pays $37,500. That is a $10,000 difference caused entirely by credit structure, not income, equity, or responsibility.

Next, look at account distribution. Jason has five cards with balances of $3,000 each. Linda has one card with $12,000 and seven cards with zero balances. The total debt is similar, but Jason has five active revolving accounts showing dependency, while Linda has only one. Mortgage-grade models penalize Jason more heavily because the behavior suggests broader reliance on credit. This pushes Jason's score even lower.

Now consider timing. Jason paid off a $5,000 card last week and saw his app score jump. But the mortgage score has not updated yet, so the HELOC lender still sees him as high risk. Linda paid down her balances two months ago, so her mortgage score fully reflects the improvement. This timing difference alone can determine whether a HELOC is approved or denied. When you add everything up, Linda gets approved for a $150,000 HELOC at 7.5 percent. Jason is capped at $50,000 at 9.5 percent. Over five years, Linda gains access to three times more capital and saves tens of thousands in interest. The math is not magic. It is simply how the scoring systems interpret risk. This is why mastering the right credit model is one of the most powerful financial skills a homeowner can learn.

Chapter 3

Revolving Credit Optimization for Maximum HELOC Limits

Revolving credit is the single most important part of your credit profile when it comes to HELOC approval and limit size. Revolving credit includes credit cards, personal lines of credit, and any account that allows you to borrow, repay, and borrow again. A HELOC is also a revolving account, which means lenders assume that your behavior with existing revolving credit predicts how you will behave with a HELOC. If you misuse or overload revolving accounts, they expect you to do the same with a home equity line. If you use them strategically and conservatively, they see you as safe to extend large amounts of capital.

The most important number in revolving credit is utilization, which is calculated by dividing your total balances by your total credit limits. If you have $40,000 in limits and $20,000 in balances, your utilization is 50 percent. Mortgage and HELOC lenders want to see utilization under 30 percent and ideally under 20 percent. Below 10 percent is considered elite. Every time your utilization rises, your risk score rises. Every time it falls, your HELOC profile strengthens. This is why paying off a card is often more powerful than opening a new one.

However, total utilization is only one layer. There is also per-card utilization. If you have one card maxed out at 90 percent and four cards at zero, your total utilization may look fine, but that maxed-out card will still damage your HELOC score. Mortgage models dislike concentrated risk. They prefer that balances be small and evenly distributed or, better yet, isolated on one low-utilization account. A borrower with $10,000 on a $50,000 card looks safer than a borrower with $10,000 on a $12,000 card, even though both owe the same amount.

Another key factor is the number of revolving accounts reporting balances. Mortgage-grade models prefer fewer active balances. If you owe $15,000, it is far better for that to be on one card than spread across five. Each card with a balance is treated as a separate risk signal. This is why balance consolidation is often a better move before a HELOC than simply paying a little on every card. Strategic placement of debt is just as important as reducing it.

Credit age also interacts with revolving credit. Old, high-limit cards with low balances are extremely powerful for HELOC underwriting. They show that you have long-term access to credit and that you do not need to use it. This is the ideal signal. New cards with high balances do the opposite. They show dependency and volatility. Before applying for a HELOC, the goal is to make your revolving credit look boring, stable, and underutilized.

Finally, lenders look at how revolving balances move over time. A borrower whose balances trend downward over six months looks safer than one whose balances bounce up and down. Even if the totals are similar, the trend matters. A declining trend signals control. A rising trend signals stress. When you prepare for a HELOC, you are not just improving your credit, you are telling a story about your financial behavior. Revolving credit is the loudest part of that story.

Practical Example

Let's compare two homeowners, Brian and Sophia, who both want a $120,000 HELOC. Brian has four credit cards with limits of $10,000 each, giving him $40,000 in total credit. He carries balances of $8,000 on each card, for a total of $32,000. His utilization is $32,000 divided by $40,000, which equals 80 percent. Sophia has six cards with limits totaling $120,000 and balances of $18,000. Her utilization is $18,000 divided by $120,000, which equals 15 percent. Right away, Sophia looks dramatically safer to a HELOC lender.

Now look at how the debt is distributed. Brian's cards are all at 80 percent utilization individually. Sophia has one card with $18,000 on a $50,000 limit, which is 36 percent, and the rest are zero. Mortgage-grade scoring models penalize Brian for having four high-risk cards, while Sophia has only one moderately used card. This difference alone could be 40 or more points on a HELOC score.

Now let's assume Brian pays $5,000 off one card. His total balance drops to $27,000. His total utilization becomes $27,000 divided by $40,000, or 67.5 percent. That is still extremely high. Sophia pays $5,000 on her card, reducing her balance to $13,000. Her utilization becomes $13,000 divided by $120,000, or 10.8 percent. That puts her into elite HELOC territory.

Because of this, Sophia qualifies for a $150,000 HELOC at 7 percent. Brian is limited to $40,000 at 10 percent. On $100,000, Sophia pays $7,000 per year in interest. Brian pays $10,000. Over five years, Brian pays $15,000 more for the same money. The only difference was how their revolving credit was structured.

This example shows that HELOC approval is not about income or equity alone. It is about how safely you manage revolving credit. When you control utilization, balance placement, and trends, you unlock cheaper, larger, and easier HELOCs.

Chapter 4

Credit Inquiries, New Accounts, and Timing Your HELOC Application

One of the most overlooked reasons HELOC applications get denied or downgraded is not because of bad credit, but because of bad timing. Credit inquiries and new accounts create what lenders call “credit velocity,” which measures how fast your financial profile is changing. Even when changes are positive, too much movement signals uncertainty. HELOC lenders want borrowers who look stable, predictable, and boring. A borrower who is constantly opening new cards, transferring balances, or shopping for loans looks like someone who might be struggling or preparing to take on risk. This is why the six to twelve months before a HELOC application are just as important as the years before it.

Every time you apply for credit, a hard inquiry appears on your report. One or two inquiries are normal, but several within a short period raise red flags. Mortgage-grade credit models penalize clusters of inquiries more heavily than consumer scores do. If you have four or five inquiries in the last six months, your HELOC score can drop 20 to 40 points even if nothing else changes. That alone can push you below approval thresholds or into higher interest tiers. The scoring system is not judging your intelligence; it is reacting to patterns that historically predict default.

New accounts create even more impact. When you open a new credit card, auto loan, or personal line, it lowers your average age of accounts and introduces uncertainty about how you will use that new credit. Mortgage and HELOC models assume that new credit will likely be used. That potential future balance is treated as risk today. This is why opening a card for a 0 percent balance transfer right before a HELOC can actually hurt your approval even if it lowers your utilization. Timing matters more than tactics.

Another issue is account seasoning. Lenders trust older accounts far more than new ones. A five-year-old card with a $30,000 limit and a $2,000 balance is incredibly powerful. A two-month-old card with a $30,000 limit and a $2,000 balance is not. Before applying for a HELOC, the goal is to let your profile age and stabilize. Ideally, you want no new accounts and no new inquiries for at least 90 days, and preferably six months.

Balance movement timing also matters. Paying down balances right before applying can help, but the mortgage-grade scoring models do not update instantly. Most lenders pull your credit using data that may be 30 to 45 days old. That means paying off a card today might not show up when the lender runs your file. This is why strategic planning is essential. The goal is not just to improve your credit, but to make sure those improvements are visible when it counts.

HELOC lenders also look at how your credit behaved leading into the application. If you were maxed out three months ago and suddenly paid everything off, the model may still see you as risky. Stability over time is more powerful than a last-minute cleanup. The best HELOC applicants look good, and have looked good, for months. That consistency is what allows lenders to offer large lines at low rates.

Practical Example

Let's look at two borrowers, Daniel and Rebecca, who both want a $100,000 HELOC. Daniel decided to "fix" his credit quickly. Three months before applying, he opened two new credit cards to increase his limits and did a balance transfer. He also applied for a personal loan to consolidate debt. In total, he generated four inquiries and three new accounts. Rebecca made no new applications for a year. She simply paid down her balances gradually.

Daniel's total limits went from $40,000 to $90,000. His balances went from $30,000 to $25,000. His utilization improved from 75 percent to 28 percent. On paper, that looks great. But the scoring model sees three new accounts and four inquiries in 90 days. His average account age drops from six years to three years. His HELOC score drops from 710 to 670 due to velocity and new account penalties.

Rebecca's limits stayed at $80,000. Her balances dropped from $24,000 to $12,000. Her utilization went from 30 percent to 15 percent. She had zero new inquiries. Her average age stayed at eight years. Her HELOC score rises from 705 to 740.

Now look at the results. Daniel is offered a $40,000 HELOC at 9.75 percent. Rebecca is approved for $150,000 at 7.25 percent. On $100,000, Daniel pays $9,750 per year. Rebecca pays $7,250. Over five years, Daniel pays $12,500 more. Even though Daniel's utilization improved more dramatically, his timing destroyed his approval power.

This example proves that when it comes to HELOCs, stability beats speed. Planning your credit moves months in advance can be worth tens of thousands of dollars in borrowing power and interest savings.

Chapter 5

How Credit Mix, Account Age, and Profile Depth Determine HELOC Power

When a HELOC lender evaluates your credit, they are not just measuring whether you are risky today. They are measuring how proven and experienced you are as a borrower. This is where credit mix, account age, and profile depth become powerful. A borrower with one credit card and one auto loan is far less predictable than a borrower with ten well-managed accounts across multiple categories. Depth and diversity give lenders statistical confidence. They show that you have successfully handled different types of debt across different economic cycles. That history reduces uncertainty, and lower uncertainty equals higher credit limits and lower interest rates.

Credit mix refers to the types of accounts you have. Revolving credit such as cards and lines of credit shows how you manage flexible borrowing. Installment credit such as mortgages, auto loans, and student loans shows how you manage fixed obligations. HELOC lenders want to see both. A borrower with only credit cards looks risky because their payments can fluctuate. A borrower with only installment loans looks rigid and less tested. The strongest profiles have both and handle them well over time.

Account age is equally important. The longer an account has existed without problems, the more trustworthy it becomes. Mortgage-grade credit models give enormous weight to the age of your oldest account and your average age. This is why closing old cards is often a mistake before a HELOC. Even if you never use a card, its age anchors your profile. Removing it can drop your HELOC score by 20 to 50 points overnight because it shortens your financial history.

Profile depth refers to how many active, well-managed accounts you have. Thin profiles with two or three accounts are fragile. One mistake or one balance spike can dramatically hurt them. Thick profiles with eight to fifteen accounts are resilient. One balance or one inquiry does not move the needle much. HELOC lenders prefer thick profiles because they behave more predictably and are statistically less likely to default.

Another key factor is how long your accounts have been active and in good standing. A borrower who opened five cards last year is not as trusted as someone who has had five cards for ten years. Time is a form of proof. It shows that you have navigated economic ups and downs without losing control. HELOC lenders lend against stability, not just numbers.

Finally, the way your accounts are distributed matters. One mortgage, one auto loan, and eight credit cards with low balances is far better than one mortgage and one credit card. The broader your financial history, the more data lenders have to trust you. This is why HELOC optimization is not just about reducing debt, but about building a strong, seasoned, diversified credit ecosystem.

Practical Example

Let's compare two homeowners, Kevin and Laura. Kevin has three accounts: one credit card with a $15,000 limit, one auto loan, and one mortgage. His credit history is four years old. Laura has ten accounts: seven credit cards with $150,000 in total limits, two auto loans, and one mortgage. Her history is fifteen years old. Both have the same income and the same home value.

Kevin owes $5,000 on his card, which is 33 percent utilization. Laura owes $20,000 across her cards, which is only 13 percent utilization. Even though Laura owes more, she has far more available credit and far more history. Kevin's HELOC score is 680. Laura's is 750.

Kevin applies for a HELOC and is offered $30,000 at 10 percent. Laura is offered $200,000 at 7 percent. On $100,000, Kevin pays $10,000 per year. Laura pays $7,000. Over five years, Laura saves $15,000. Now look at what happens if Kevin closes his oldest credit card to "simplify." His history drops from four years to two years. His score drops another 30 points. He is now below many HELOC minimums. Laura, who kept her oldest accounts open, continues to qualify easily.

This shows that building and preserving credit depth is one of the most powerful HELOC strategies available. When lenders trust your history, they trust your future.

Chapter 6

How Credit Behavior Over Time Predicts HELOC Risk and Pricing

HELOC lenders are not just looking at where your credit is today, they are studying how it has behaved over time. Credit history is not a snapshot; it is a movie. Every payment, every balance change, every inquiry, and every account opening becomes part of a behavioral pattern that tells lenders how you are likely to handle access to large amounts of revolving capital. Two borrowers with identical credit scores can receive completely different HELOC offers simply because one has a stable, predictable history and the other has a volatile one. Stability is the most valuable asset in underwriting.

One of the most important behavioral signals is balance trend. A borrower whose revolving balances have steadily declined over the last six to twelve months is seen as reducing risk. A borrower whose balances have increased or fluctuated is seen as becoming riskier, even if the current balance is acceptable. Lenders know that people who are climbing out of debt are far more likely to manage new credit responsibly than those who are sliding deeper into it. This trend is built directly into mortgage-grade scoring models. Payment history also has depth. It is not just whether you have ever missed a payment, but how recently and how often. A late payment three years ago is far less damaging than one last month. A borrower with one late five years ago looks stable. A borrower with three late payments in the last year looks dangerous. HELOC lenders are particularly sensitive to recent behavior because they are offering you flexible, ongoing access to cash.

Another powerful signal is utilization trend. If your utilization was 70 percent six months ago and is now 20 percent, that tells a story of improving financial control. If it was 20 percent and is now 60 percent, that tells the opposite story. Even if both borrowers have 40 percent today, their past trajectories create very different risk profiles. Lenders price HELOCs based on where they think you are going, not just where you are.

The length of time you maintain low utilization and on-time payments also matters. A borrower who has been under 20 percent utilization for a year looks far safer than someone who just dropped below 20 percent last week. Time smooths out noise. This is why preparation for a HELOC should begin months in advance, not days.

Finally, HELOC lenders use these behavioral trends to determine not only approval but interest rate, credit limit, and draw period terms. A stable borrower might receive a higher line, a longer draw period, and a lower rate. A volatile borrower might be approved but capped, charged more, or given restrictive terms. Credit behavior is not just a gatekeeper. It is a pricing engine.

Practical Example

Let's look at two borrowers, Ethan and Monica, who both apply for a $120,000 HELOC. Six months ago, Ethan had $50,000 in credit card limits and $35,000 in balances, which is 70 percent utilization. Over the next six months, he paid down $2,000 per month. After six months, he now owes $23,000. His utilization is $23,000 divided by $50,000, or 46 percent. That is still high, but it is trending down.

Monica also had $50,000 in limits six months ago, but only $10,000 in balances, which is 20 percent utilization. Over six months, she used cards for expenses and now owes $25,000. Her utilization is $25,000 divided by $50,000, or 50 percent. Today, Ethan is at 46 percent and Monica is at 50 percent. On the surface, Ethan looks better.

However, lenders look at the trend. Ethan went from 70 percent to 46 percent, a 24-point improvement. Monica went from 20 percent to 50 percent, a 30-point decline. Ethan is becoming safer. Monica is becoming riskier. Even though Monica used to be in better shape, her recent behavior is negative. Now factor in pricing. Ethan is approved for $120,000 at 8 percent. Monica is approved for only $60,000 at 10 percent. On $60,000, Monica pays $6,000 per year in interest. Ethan pays $9,600 on $120,000. Per dollar borrowed, Monica is paying more because her risk trend is worse.

Over five years, Ethan pays $48,000 in interest on $120,000. Monica pays $30,000 on $60,000. If Monica had maintained her low utilization, she could have borrowed twice as much at a lower rate. The difference was not her past. It was her recent behavior. This is why credit trends are one of the most powerful levers in HELOC strategy.

Chapter 7

How HELOC Lenders Combine Credit with Equity and Income

No HELOC is approved on credit alone. Credit is powerful, but it is only one leg of a three-part decision. The other two legs are home equity and income. A borrower can have perfect credit and still be denied if the equity or income profile creates too much risk. Likewise, a borrower with average credit can sometimes be approved for large HELOCs because their equity and income reduce the lender's exposure. Understanding how these three forces interact allows you to position yourself far more intelligently than someone who focuses on credit score alone.

Home equity is measured by loan-to-value, or LTV. LTV is calculated by dividing your total mortgage balances by your home's current value. If your home is worth $500,000 and you owe $250,000, your LTV is 50 percent. Most HELOC lenders have maximum combined LTV limits between 80 percent and 90 percent. That means in this example, the maximum total debt allowed would be between $400,000 and $450,000. Subtract the $250,000 mortgage and you could potentially borrow $150,000 to $200,000 on a HELOC. The lower your LTV, the safer you are to the lender. That safety can offset weaker credit.

Income is measured by debt-to-income ratio, or DTI. DTI is calculated by dividing your total monthly debt payments by your gross monthly income. If you earn $10,000 per month and have $3,000 in debt payments, your DTI is 30 percent. Most HELOC lenders want DTI below 43 percent, and the best pricing is usually reserved for borrowers below 36 percent. Lower DTI means more room to absorb the HELOC payment without financial strain. Again, this can compensate for credit imperfections.

Credit then ties these together. A borrower with 50 percent LTV and 30 percent DTI might qualify for a HELOC even with a 680 score. A borrower with 85 percent LTV and 45 percent DTI might be denied even with a 740 score. Lenders are not judging you on one metric. They are judging how much cushion they have if something goes wrong. The more cushion you provide through equity and income, the more flexible they become on credit.

HELOC pricing also responds to this blend. A borrower with excellent credit but high LTV may get approved but at a higher rate. A borrower with average credit and very low LTV may get a surprisingly low rate. This is because the lender's true risk is the chance of loss. Equity reduces loss severity. Income reduces default probability. Credit predicts behavior. Together, they create the final offer.

This is why HELOC strategy should be holistic. Improving credit without improving equity or DTI only goes so far. Increasing equity through appreciation or paying down the mortgage can dramatically increase HELOC power. Increasing income or reducing other debts can do the same. When you understand this triangle, you can choose the most efficient lever to pull to get the HELOC you want.

Practical Example

Let's compare two homeowners, Thomas and Elena. Thomas has a home worth $600,000 and owes $420,000. His LTV is $420,000 divided by $600,000, or 70 percent. Elena has a home worth $600,000 and owes $300,000. Her LTV is 50 percent. Both apply for a HELOC with an 85 percent combined LTV limit. Thomas can go up to $510,000 total debt, so his maximum HELOC is $90,000. Elena can go up to $510,000, so her maximum HELOC is $210,000.

Now look at income. Thomas earns $8,000 per month and has $3,500 in existing debt payments, giving him a DTI of 43.75 percent. Elena earns $10,000 per month and has $2,500 in payments, giving her a DTI of 25 percent. Elena has far more room for a HELOC payment.

Thomas has a 730 credit score. Elena has a 690. Even though Thomas has better credit, Elena is approved for a $200,000 HELOC at 7.5 percent. Thomas is approved for only $60,000 at 9 percent. On $60,000, Thomas pays $5,400 per year. On $200,000, Elena pays $15,000. But Elena has access to over three times the capital at a lower rate because her equity and income made her safer.

This shows that HELOC power is not just about credit. It is about how credit, equity, and income combine. When you control all three, you control your borrowing destiny.

Chapter 8

Building a Pre-HELOC Credit Optimization Plan

Getting approved for a large, low-interest HELOC is not something that happens by accident. It is the result of deliberate, planned credit behavior carried out over months. The biggest mistake homeowners make is waiting until they "need" a HELOC and then trying to fix their credit in a rush. By that time, their credit profile is already locked in by past behavior, and most of the changes they make will not show up in time. The correct approach is to treat your HELOC like a business project, with a preparation phase, a stabilization phase, and an execution phase.

The first step in a pre-HELOC optimization plan is to freeze credit activity. That means no new credit cards, no auto loans, no personal loans, and no unnecessary inquiries for at least 90 days and preferably six months before applying. Every new account or inquiry injects uncertainty into your profile. Even a good move, such as opening a card to lower utilization, can hurt in the short term because it lowers average age and signals financial motion. Stability is the most valuable asset you can present to a HELOC lender. The second step is to restructure revolving balances. This is where most of the power comes from. The goal is to reduce total utilization below 30 percent and ideally below 20 percent, while also minimizing the number of cards carrying balances. This usually means consolidating balances onto one or two high-limit cards and aggressively paying them down. It also means keeping old, high-limit cards open even if you never use them. These accounts act as credit anchors that boost your score and lower your utilization ratio.

The third step is to create a clean payment trend. That means no late payments, no missed payments, and no sudden spikes in balances. Even one 30-day late in the three months before a HELOC can destroy approval odds. The goal is to show lenders that your finances are boring and predictable. Automatic payments and consistent reductions in balances are key tools here.

The fourth step is timing. Because mortgage-grade credit scores lag behind consumer scores, you must complete most of your credit optimization at least 45 to 60 days before applying. This ensures that when the lender pulls your report, it reflects your improved utilization and stability. A last-minute payoff might make you feel better, but it might not help your HELOC.

Finally, the plan must be aligned with your equity and income. If your loan-to-value or debt-to-income ratios are tight, you may need to pay down your mortgage or other debts as part of the preparation. Credit optimization alone cannot overcome structural limits. When all three elements are aligned, you create a powerful HELOC profile that attracts large lines and low rates.

Practical Example

Let's look at how this works in real life. Imagine a homeowner named Rachel who wants a $150,000 HELOC in six months. Today, she has $60,000 in credit card limits and $30,000 in balances. Her utilization is $30,000 divided by $60,000, or 50 percent. She has four cards with balances and two with zero. Her mortgage-grade score is 670, which is too low for the best HELOC programs.

Rachel creates a six-month plan. In month one, she stops all new credit applications. In months one through four, she pays $3,000 per month toward her cards, for a total of $12,000. Her balances drop from $30,000 to $18,000. Her utilization becomes $18,000 divided by $60,000, or 30 percent. In months five and six, she pays another $2,000 per month, dropping balances to $14,000. Her utilization becomes $14,000 divided by $60,000, or 23 percent.

She also consolidates all balances onto two high-limit cards, leaving four cards at zero. This reduces the number of active revolving accounts from four to two, which further boosts her HELOC score. By month five, her mortgage-grade score rises from 670 to 710. By month six, it reaches 725.

Now she applies. Because she prepared early, the lender's credit pull reflects the lower balances and the stable trend. She is approved for a $160,000 HELOC at 7.25 percent instead of being denied or capped at $40,000 at 10 percent.

On $150,000, 7.25 percent interest is $10,875 per year. At 10 percent, it would have been $15,000. Over five years, her planning saves her over $20,000 in interest and gives her access to four times more capital. The math is simple. The strategy is powerful. This is what intentional HELOC preparation looks like.

Chapter 9

Avoiding Credit Pitfalls That Kill HELOC Approvals

Many homeowners fail to qualify for a HELOC not because their finances are truly weak, but because they unknowingly trigger risk signals that lenders are trained to avoid. These credit pitfalls often feel harmless on the surface, but inside underwriting systems they are interpreted as warning signs of future instability. Understanding what these traps are and how to avoid them is one of the most powerful ways to protect your borrowing power.

One of the most damaging pitfalls is carrying high revolving utilization, even if you pay on time. From a consumer's point of view, making minimum payments and never missing one feels responsible. From a HELOC lender's point of view, it looks like slow-motion financial distress. High utilization means you are relying heavily on borrowed money to operate your life. That means if your income drops or expenses spike, you have no cushion. This is why lenders penalize high balances far more than most people realize.

Another major pitfall is opening or closing accounts too close to a HELOC application. Opening new cards lowers your average account age and increases uncertainty. Closing old cards removes valuable history and increases utilization. Both actions make you look riskier, even if your intentions are good. Many people close old cards to "clean up" their credit before applying, not realizing they are destroying one of their strongest assets.

Late payments, even small ones, are also devastating. A single 30-day late within the last 12 months can drop your mortgage-grade score by 50 points or more. HELOC lenders assume that recent late payments predict future ones. Even if you explain the reason, the model does not care. It only sees probability.

Another subtle pitfall is carrying balances across many cards instead of one or two. This makes you look dependent on revolving credit. It also increases the number of negative risk signals on your report. Consolidating balances reduces this noise and makes your profile look cleaner and more controlled.

Finally, many borrowers sabotage themselves by trying to "game" the system too quickly. They pay off large balances right before applying, open new cards to increase limits, or move money around aggressively. These moves create volatility, and volatility is treated as risk. The goal is not to look perfect for one day. The goal is to look stable for many months.

Practical Example

Consider a borrower named Mike. Mike has a home worth $500,000 and owes $250,000, so he has plenty of equity. He wants a $100,000 HELOC. His credit cards have $50,000 in limits and $30,000 in balances, which is 60 percent utilization. He decides to "clean up" his credit two weeks before applying. He pays off $10,000, lowering his balances to $20,000 and utilization to 40 percent. He also closes two old cards he never uses.

Because he closed those cards, his total limits drop from $50,000 to $30,000. His $20,000 balance is now 66 percent utilization. Even though he paid $10,000, he actually made his profile worse. His mortgage-grade score drops from 690 to 660. He is denied.

Now consider Sarah. She also has $50,000 in limits and $30,000 in balances. Six months before applying, she begins paying $3,000 per month. After six months, she owes $12,000. Her utilization is $12,000 divided by $50,000, or 24 percent. She keeps all old cards open. Her mortgage-grade score rises from 680 to 730. She is approved for a $120,000 HELOC at 7.5 percent. Mike's last-minute actions cost him approval. Sarah's patience earned her tens of thousands in borrowing power. The math is simple, but the discipline is what makes the difference.

Chapter 10

The Complete Credit Blueprint for Maximum HELOC Power

At this point in the Home Equity Wealth Series, you now understand that HELOC approval is not random, and it is not based on a single number. It is the result of a complete credit ecosystem that tells lenders how you behave with money, how stable you are over time, and how much risk they take by extending you revolving access to large amounts of capital. This chapter brings everything together into one unified blueprint you can follow to design your HELOC profile intentionally instead of hoping for a good outcome.

The first pillar of the blueprint is utilization control. This means keeping total revolving utilization below 30 percent, ideally below 20 percent, and never letting any individual card exceed 50 percent of its limit. This creates both global and per-account safety signals. It also means concentrating balances on one or two large, old cards while leaving the rest at zero. This reduces the number of risk signals and improves mortgage-grade scoring. Utilization is not just about debt, it is about how close you are to your limits. Limits are your buffer. Buffers are what lenders trust. The second pillar is stability over time. This includes no late payments, no collections, no charge-offs, and no sudden spikes in balances. It also means no new credit accounts or inquiries for at least 90 days and preferably six months before applying. Your credit should look calm and predictable. The quieter your report looks, the safer you appear to a HELOC underwriter.

The third pillar is depth and age. Keep your oldest accounts open, even if you never use them. Maintain a mix of installment and revolving credit. Aim for at least eight active accounts with a long average age. This creates a thick, resilient profile that can absorb small changes without collapsing. Thin profiles are fragile. Thick profiles are powerful.

The fourth pillar is alignment with equity and income. Credit does not exist in isolation. If your loan-to-value is high, your credit must be excellent. If your debt-to-income is tight, your credit must be strong. If your equity and income are exceptional, your credit can be average and still work. The blueprint requires you to balance all three.

The final pillar is timing and execution. You do not optimize credit the week before you apply. You build it over months, allow it to season, and then apply when your numbers and trends are at their best. This is how professionals do it. When you follow this blueprint, HELOC approval becomes predictable instead of stressful.

Practical Example

Let's walk through a complete HELOC credit blueprint in action. Imagine a homeowner named Victor who wants a $200,000 HELOC. His home is worth $700,000 and he owes $350,000, giving him 50 percent LTV. That means he can go up to 85 percent combined LTV, or $595,000 total debt. Subtract $350,000 and he has room for $245,000 in a HELOC. Equity is not the problem. Credit is.

Victor has $80,000 in credit card limits and $40,000 in balances, which is 50 percent utilization. His mortgage-grade score is 675. Over six months, he pays $5,000 per month. After six months, he owes $10,000. His utilization becomes $10,000 divided by $80,000, or 12.5 percent. He also consolidates the $10,000 onto one old $40,000 card, leaving the rest at zero.

He opens no new accounts and has no inquiries during this time. His average age stays at nine years. His score rises from 675 to 735. His DTI drops because his credit card payments fall from $1,200 per month to $300.

Now Victor applies. With a 735 HELOC score, 50 percent LTV, and lower DTI, he is approved for $220,000 at 7 percent. On $200,000, he pays $14,000 per year in interest. If he had applied earlier at 675, he would have been capped at $75,000 at 10 percent, paying $7,500 per year for far less capital.

By following the blueprint, Victor unlocked nearly three times more money at a lower cost. That is the power of credit mastery.

Chapter 11

How to Maintain HELOC-Ready Credit After You're Approved

Many homeowners believe that once their HELOC is approved, the credit work is finished. In reality, that is when the real responsibility begins. A HELOC is not a one-time loan; it is a living financial instrument that remains open for years. During that time, lenders continue to monitor your credit behavior, and your actions can affect your interest rate, your available credit, and even whether your line remains open. Understanding how to stay HELOC-ready after approval protects the financial power you worked so hard to build.

One of the most important rules after receiving a HELOC is to keep your revolving utilization low, even when you start using the line. A HELOC increases your total available credit, which can help your credit score if you do not abuse it. But if you draw a large balance and also allow your credit cards to climb, you can push your overall utilization into dangerous territory. The goal is to treat the HELOC as a strategic tool, not as a replacement for credit cards. If you draw \$50,000 on a \$200,000 HELOC, your HELOC utilization is only 25 percent, which is healthy. But if you also carry high balances on cards, the combined picture can look risky.

Payment behavior becomes even more important once a HELOC is active. Late payments on a HELOC are treated very harshly by credit models because they involve large sums and secured collateral. One 30-day late can drop your score by 60 points or more and can trigger account reviews by the lender. Automatic payments and strong cash flow buffers are essential. You should never rely on memory to manage a HELOC payment.

Another critical factor is how you manage your credit cards after getting a HELOC. Many people use the HELOC to pay off cards, which is a powerful strategy if done correctly. But once those cards are paid off, they must remain mostly unused. If you pay off $30,000 of cards with a HELOC and then run the cards back up again, you have doubled your risk. Lenders watch for this pattern, and it can result in line freezes or credit limit reductions.

HELOC lenders also periodically review credit profiles. They look at utilization, payment history, and new accounts. If they see deteriorating credit, they may reduce your available line or change your pricing. This is not personal. It is risk management. The safest way to protect your HELOC is to keep your credit boring: low utilization, few inquiries, no new risky accounts, and consistent payments. Finally, maintaining HELOC-ready credit allows you to use your home equity repeatedly. A well-managed HELOC can be drawn down, paid off, and drawn again over many years. Each cycle gives you access to capital for investing, debt elimination, or business growth. But this only works if your credit remains strong. Your HELOC is only as powerful as the profile that supports it.

Practical Example

Let's look at how this works with real numbers. Imagine a homeowner named Alicia who is approved for a $200,000 HELOC. She also has $100,000 in total credit card limits and $20,000 in card balances. Before the HELOC, her utilization was $20,000 divided by $100,000, or 20 percent. After the HELOC is added, her total available credit becomes $300,000. If she keeps her $20,000 in card balances and does not draw on the HELOC, her utilization becomes $20,000 divided by $300,000, or 6.7 percent. Her credit score rises because she now has more unused credit.

Alicia uses $50,000 from the HELOC to pay off $20,000 in cards and fund a small investment. Her new balances are $50,000 on the HELOC and $0 on cards. Her utilization is $50,000 divided by $300,000, or 16.7 percent, which is still very healthy. She now pays interest only on the $50,000, not the full $200,000 line. If her HELOC rate is 7 percent, her annual interest is $3,500.

Now imagine she makes a mistake and runs her cards back up to $25,000. Her total balances become $75,000. Her utilization becomes $75,000 divided by $300,000, or 25 percent. That is still manageable, but the lender sees rising dependency. If she pushes cards to $60,000 while still owing $50,000 on the HELOC, her balances become $110,000 and utilization becomes $110,000 divided by $300,000, or 36.7 percent. That puts her into a risk zone.

At 36.7 percent utilization, her score drops, and the lender may reduce her available HELOC from $150,000 remaining to $80,000. By contrast, if she keeps cards at zero and pays the HELOC down steadily, she can preserve her full $200,000 access for years.

This example shows that HELOC success is not just about getting approved. It is about maintaining discipline so that the line stays open, affordable, and available whenever you need it.

Chapter 12

Using Credit Mastery to Build Long-Term Home Equity Wealth

Credit mastery is not simply a tool for getting approved for a HELOC. It is the foundation of long-term financial control. When used correctly, your credit profile becomes the engine that allows your home equity to be deployed, recovered, and redeployed over and over again in a disciplined wealth-building cycle. Most homeowners use home equity once, usually for a renovation or an emergency. Wealthy homeowners use it repeatedly, safely, and strategically. The difference is not income or luck. It is credit discipline.

When your credit is optimized, lenders view you as a low-risk steward of capital. That allows you to access larger lines, lower rates, and more flexible terms. Those advantages compound. Lower interest means more of every dollar you borrow can go toward productive uses instead of lender profit. Larger lines mean you can act quickly when opportunities appear. Flexible draw periods mean you can time your investments instead of rushing them. Credit mastery turns your house into a revolving investment engine. The key to long-term success is never letting your credit profile deteriorate while you use your HELOC. That means maintaining low utilization, strong payment history, and minimal new credit activity. When you borrow, you must always have a plan for how the borrowed money will return to you. Whether you use a HELOC for real estate, business, or debt elimination, the goal is to create cash flow or savings that exceed the interest you pay. This positive spread is what grows wealth.

Another critical principle is equity preservation. Just because a lender will let you borrow up to 85 or 90 percent LTV does not mean you should. Smart borrowers leave a safety buffer. This protects you from market downturns and keeps you in control of your home. A HELOC is a tool, not a license to gamble. The best long-term users operate between 50 and 70 percent LTV whenever possible.

Over time, a disciplined borrower can use the same HELOC to fund multiple projects. You draw money, deploy it, generate returns, pay the line back down, and repeat. Each cycle builds experience, confidence, and financial strength. Your credit remains strong because you never let utilization spiral out of control. Your equity grows because you use borrowed money productively.

This is the final transformation. You stop being a homeowner who hopes their house goes up in value, and become an equity strategist who actively grows wealth. Credit mastery is the gateway to that world.

Practical Example

Let's see how this works with real numbers. Imagine a homeowner named Daniel with a $600,000 home and a $300,000 mortgage. His LTV is 50 percent. He qualifies for a $200,000 HELOC, but he chooses to only use $100,000 to stay conservative.

Daniel uses the $100,000 to buy and renovate a small rental property that nets $1,500 per month after expenses. His HELOC interest rate is 7 percent, so on $100,000 he pays $7,000 per year, or about $583 per month. His cash flow after paying HELOC interest is $1,500 minus $583, which equals $917 per month, or $11,004 per year.

Daniel uses that $11,004 to pay down the HELOC. After one year, his balance drops from $100,000 to $88,996. His utilization remains low because his HELOC limit is $200,000 and his cards are at zero. His credit stays strong.

In year two, he repeats the process. He still earns about $11,000 from the rental. He pays the HELOC down to roughly $78,000. After three years, the balance is around $67,000. At that point, he has recovered $33,000 of his original capital and still owns the rental. Daniel can now draw another $30,000 to invest again while staying under 50 percent utilization of his HELOC. Over time, his home equity and income grow together. He is not getting richer by chance. He is doing it by design.

This is what credit mastery makes possible.

Chapter 13

Turning Your HELOC Into a Permanent Financial Control System

By the time you reach this point in the Home Equity Wealth Series, you should no longer see a HELOC as a loan. A HELOC is a control system. It is a financial command center that allows you to decide when, where, and how your capital moves. Most people live at the mercy of fixed paychecks, high-interest credit cards, and slow-moving banks. When your credit is mastered and your HELOC is structured correctly, you operate from a position of liquidity, flexibility, and strategic advantage. That is the true power of this tool.

A permanent financial control system is built on three principles: liquidity, timing, and leverage. Liquidity means having access to capital when opportunities or emergencies arise without having to beg, sell, or wait. A HELOC provides that liquidity at a fraction of the cost of credit cards or personal loans. Timing means being able to act when prices are low, when investments appear, or when debts can be eliminated cheaply. Without access to cash, timing is irrelevant. Leverage means using other people's money at a low cost to accelerate what you can do with your own. When used responsibly, leverage allows you to grow faster without increasing personal risk.

To turn a HELOC into a permanent control system, you must operate it like a professional. That means always knowing your balances, your utilization, and your repayment schedule. It means never allowing the line to drift into chaos. The HELOC should be treated like a working capital account, not a piggy bank. Money flows out to productive uses and flows back in from income, savings, or returns. The cycle never stops.

Credit discipline remains the backbone of the system. If your credit deteriorates, your HELOC becomes vulnerable. Lines can be frozen, limits can be reduced, and pricing can increase. When your credit remains strong, your HELOC becomes a long-term asset that can be used for decades. This is how sophisticated borrowers build financial resilience that survives recessions, job changes, and market cycles.

Another powerful aspect of a HELOC control system is optionality. Because you have access to capital, you can choose between paying cash, borrowing, or waiting. You can refinance debt, buy assets, or bridge temporary gaps without panic. That freedom alone is worth more than the interest you pay.

Ultimately, this is what separates financially secure homeowners from financially stressed ones. They are not richer because they earn more. They are stronger because they control their liquidity. A well-managed HELOC, supported by mastered credit, becomes the foundation of that control.

Practical Example

Let's see how a HELOC becomes a control system in real life. Imagine a homeowner named Maria with a $700,000 home and a $350,000 mortgage. Her LTV is 50 percent. She is approved for a $250,000 HELOC but uses only $80,000 at any given time to stay conservative.

Maria earns $12,000 per month and has $4,000 in expenses. That leaves $8,000 in surplus cash flow. She uses her HELOC to pay for major expenses, investments, and opportunities, then uses her income to pay it back. For example, she uses $40,000 to buy a discounted vehicle instead of financing it at 9 percent. She pays it off over 10 months by sending $4,000 per month back to the HELOC. At 7 percent interest, the $40,000 costs her about $2,800 in interest over that period, far less than a traditional loan.

She also uses $30,000 from the HELOC to invest in a small business that returns $1,000 per month. That income flows back to the HELOC, paying it down. In 30 months, the $30,000 is fully recovered, but the business continues producing income. At any time, Maria's utilization stays below 32 percent because her line is $250,000 and her balance is under $80,000. Her credit remains strong. Her liquidity remains high. If an emergency arises or an opportunity appears, she has capital ready.

This is not debt. This is control.

Chapter 14

The Long-Term Exit Strategy: Using Credit to Retire Debt and Secure Wealth

The ultimate purpose of mastering credit and using a HELOC is not to borrow forever, but to create a path that leads you out of debt and into permanent financial security. A well-designed exit strategy allows you to use leverage while you are building wealth and then gradually unwind that leverage so that your home becomes free and clear and your income is no longer dependent on borrowing. Most people never think about how they will exit debt. They simply hope that someday it will be gone. Professionals plan their exit from the beginning.

The first step of a long-term exit strategy is understanding that not all debt is equal. High-interest consumer debt such as credit cards, personal loans, and retail financing destroys wealth. Low-interest, flexible debt such as a HELOC, when used carefully, can accelerate wealth building. The goal is to convert bad debt into strategic debt, and then convert strategic debt into zero debt over time. This process starts by using the HELOC to eliminate expensive obligations, reducing the total amount of interest you pay each year. Once high-interest debt is eliminated, the next phase is to use the HELOC only for productive purposes that either generate income or increase your net worth. This could include rental properties, business investments, or value-adding improvements to your home. Each dollar borrowed must have a plan to return to you with a surplus. That surplus is what pays the HELOC down and eventually frees you from it.

A critical part of the exit strategy is maintaining conservative loan-to-value levels. Even if a lender allows you to borrow up to 85 or 90 percent of your home's value, a disciplined borrower aims to stay much lower, often below 65 percent. This protects you from market downturns and ensures that you always have equity left when it is time to exit. The goal is to be in control of your home, not dependent on it.

As your investments and income grow, you gradually reduce reliance on the HELOC. You begin to pay it down not just from profits, but from increased cash flow. Eventually, the HELOC becomes a backup tool instead of a daily driver. At that point, you can choose to close it, refinance into a fixed loan, or simply leave it unused as a safety net.

The endgame is simple: a paid-off home, strong credit, and multiple streams of income that no longer require leverage. Credit mastery gives you the ability to use debt intelligently on the way up and remove it on the way out. That is how you turn a house into a permanent source of security instead of stress.

Practical Example

Let's walk through a full exit strategy using real numbers. Imagine a homeowner named Victor who has a $600,000 home and a $300,000 mortgage. He opens a $150,000 HELOC and uses $60,000 to pay off credit cards and personal loans that were costing him 18 percent interest. Those debts were costing him $10,800 per year in interest. The HELOC costs him 7 percent, or $4,200 per year on $60,000. That saves him $6,600 per year immediately.

Victor also uses $40,000 from the HELOC to invest in a rental property that produces $900 per month in cash flow, or $10,800 per year. After paying $2,800 in HELOC interest on that $40,000, he nets $8,000. He uses that $8,000 plus the $6,600 in interest savings to pay down the HELOC by $14,600 per year.

After four years, Victor has paid down $58,400 of his HELOC. His balance drops from $100,000 to $41,600. During that time, his rental property continues producing income. At that point, he can either pay off the remaining balance or leave it as a small, low-risk line.

Victor now has no credit card debt, a profitable rental, and a nearly paid-off HELOC. His mortgage remains, but his net worth and cash flow are far higher than when he started. This is what a planned exit looks like.

Chapter 15

The Homeowner's Credit Commandment: Rules for Lifetime HELOC Power

When you reach this final stage of credit mastery, the objective is no longer just to qualify for a HELOC or even to use it profitably. The objective is to create rules that protect your financial power for life. These are the commandments that ensure your credit, your home equity, and your borrowing ability never fall back into chaos. Most people lose financial ground not because they make one big mistake, but because they slowly drift away from discipline. A permanent set of rules eliminates that drift.

The first commandment is to never let revolving utilization exceed 30 percent for more than a short period, and never let it exceed 50 percent at all. This rule alone protects your credit score, your lender trust, and your borrowing power. When you allow utilization to climb too high, you signal dependency. When you keep it low, you signal control. Control is what lenders reward.

The second commandment is to never miss a payment. Not on a credit card, not on a HELOC, not on anything. One late payment can undo years of good behavior. Automatic payments, large cash buffers, and conservative spending are the tools that make this rule easy to follow. If you ever feel stretched, the solution is to reduce usage, not to gamble on timing.

The third commandment is to preserve your credit history. Old accounts are gold. They should be protected, even if you never use them. Closing an old card is like deleting part of your financial identity. A long, clean history is one of the strongest signals of trustworthiness you can have.

The fourth commandment is to use debt only with a return plan. Every dollar borrowed must have a reason and a path back. Borrowing for consumption weakens your future. Borrowing for income, growth, or efficiency strengthens it. This rule is what separates leverage from liability.

The fifth commandment is to keep your loan-to-value conservative. Just because you can borrow up to 85 or 90 percent does not mean you should. Staying below 65 percent gives you safety, flexibility, and peace of mind. Equity is not something to gamble. It is something to guard.

When these commandments are followed, your HELOC becomes a permanent financial asset rather than a temporary loan. Your credit becomes a tool rather than a trap. And your home becomes the foundation of long-term wealth instead of a source of stress.

Practical Example

Let's see how these commandments protect a real homeowner. Imagine a borrower named Linda with a $700,000 home and a $300,000 mortgage. She has a $200,000 HELOC but never uses more than $80,000. That keeps her utilization at 40 percent on the HELOC and far lower when combined with her credit cards, which are at zero.

She uses $50,000 of the HELOC to buy a small business that pays her $1,200 per month. The interest on $50,000 at 7 percent is $3,500 per year, or about $292 per month. Her net profit is $908 per month, or $10,896 per year. She uses that money to pay down the HELOC.

After five years, she has paid off over $54,000, which means her HELOC balance is now close to zero, but she still owns the business. Her home equity remains strong, her credit remains high, and her borrowing power remains intact.

If Linda had ignored the commandments and maxed out her HELOC or run up her cards, she might have lost her line or been trapped by payments. Instead, she created a system that grows stronger with time. That is the power of lifetime credit mastery.

Final Thoughts

Credit Mastery for HELOC Approval

Credit mastery is not about impressing banks, chasing scores, or fitting into someone else's financial mold. It is about reclaiming control over how money flows through your life. Throughout this book, you have learned that your credit profile is not a reflection of your worth or your intelligence, but a set of data points that lenders use to measure risk. Once you understand how those data points work, you stop being at their mercy. You begin to shape them intentionally. That shift alone changes everything. Instead of hoping for approval, you now know how to engineer it.

Home equity is one of the most powerful financial assets most families will ever own, yet most never learn how to access it safely, efficiently, or strategically. They either ignore it or misuse it. Credit mastery is what allows you to unlock that equity without putting your home at risk. By managing utilization, timing, account structure, and behavior trends, you can make lenders view you as a low-risk steward of capital. That perception translates into higher limits, lower interest rates, and far more financial flexibility.

What makes a HELOC different from other loans is that it is not just a transaction; it is a relationship. It remains open for years. It evolves as your credit evolves. It responds to your behavior. When your credit improves, your HELOC becomes more powerful. When your credit deteriorates, it becomes more fragile. That is why this book does not just teach you how to get approved, but how to stay approved. Long-term success with home equity is built on consistency, not one-time actions.

You now understand that small choices have big consequences. A single late payment, a few maxed-out cards, or a cluster of new accounts can cost you tens of thousands of dollars in lost borrowing power. On the other hand, a few months of discipline, a few strategic payments, and a little patience can unlock more capital than most people ever realize is possible. This is not magic. It is math. It is probability. And now it is in your hands.

The most important lesson is that credit is not something you "have." It is something you manage. Every decision you make either strengthens or weakens your financial position. When you choose to keep utilization low, preserve old accounts, and move slowly and deliberately, you are building a foundation that will support you for decades. When you choose chaos and impulse, you are eroding that foundation. The difference between financial stress and financial freedom is often nothing more than credit discipline applied over time. As a licensed mortgage broker, I have seen firsthand what happens when people take control of their credit. I have watched families erase crushing debt, fund businesses, buy investment properties, and create income streams that changed their lives. I have also seen what happens when credit is ignored. The same house that could have been a financial engine becomes a financial prison. The difference is knowledge and strategy. You now have both.

Your home is not just where you live. It is a storehouse of potential. Your credit is the key that unlocks it. Used wisely, they can provide security, opportunity, and peace of mind for the rest of your life. This book has given you the blueprint. The next step is simply to apply it with patience, discipline, and intention. When you do, you will discover that financial freedom is not a dream. It is a system.

How to Get a Personalized HELOC Review

If you found *HELOC Fundamentals: How Home Equity Lines of Credit Really Work — and How to Use Them Safely* helpful, you may want to see how these concepts apply to your own home, credit profile, and financial goals.

Every homeowner's situation is unique. Home value, mortgage balance, credit history, income type, and state-specific lending rules all affect how much equity you can access, what type of HELOC you may qualify for, and what terms may be available. The examples in this book are designed to teach how HELOCs work — but your real options can only be determined by reviewing your actual numbers.

If you would like a **no-obligation Home Equity Line of Credit review**, you can request one here:

Website:https://www.nodocsheloc.com

Email:info@FinibiMortgage.com

A licensed mortgage broker will review your information and explain what HELOC and home equity options may be available to you based on your specific situation.

No cost. No pressure. No obligation.

Joseph G. Correa

About the Author

Joseph G. Correa is a licensed mortgage broker and the founder of Finibi Mortgage, a Florida-based brokerage specializing in home equity, real estate investment financing, and alternative lending strategies for homeowners, business owners, and investors. With more than two decades of experience in mortgage lending, underwriting, and financial structuring, Joseph has helped thousands of borrowers access capital using intelligent, low-risk leverage rather than high-interest consumer debt.

Unlike traditional loan officers who focus only on closing transactions, Joseph's approach is rooted in long-term financial strategy. He believes that mortgages, HELOCs, and credit lines should be used as tools for building wealth, protecting cash flow, and creating financial resilience — not as traps that keep families locked into decades of unnecessary interest payments. This philosophy has made him a trusted advisor for entrepreneurs, real estate investors, and self-employed borrowers who need flexible, modern financing solutions that banks often fail to provide.

Joseph is widely known for his expertise in home equity lines of credit, no-documentation and bank-statement loan programs, investor financing, and creative equity-based strategies such as debt-elimination systems and capital recycling. His ability to translate complex lending rules into simple, actionable guidance has helped homeowners turn idle equity into productive capital for investments, businesses, and passive income.

Through his education platform, Finibi Academy, Joseph has trained tens of thousands of students worldwide in credit, mortgage strategy, real estate financing, and financial independence. His courses and books are used by first-time homeowners, seasoned investors, and financial professionals seeking a clearer, more honest understanding of how modern lending really works.

Joseph created *The Home Equity Wealth Series* to give everyday homeowners the same financial knowledge that banks, hedge funds, and institutional investors use to control capital and minimize risk. His mission is simple: to help people stop guessing, stop fearing debt, and start using smart leverage to build real financial freedom.

When he is not structuring loans or writing, Joseph works with families and investors across the United States to design personalized equity strategies that align with their goals, cash flow, and long-term wealth plans.

The Home Equity Wealth Series Roadmap

The Professional Guide to Using Your Home to Build Financial Freedom

The purpose of *The Home Equity Wealth Series* is to give homeowners the same financial tools and strategies used by banks, investors, and institutions—translated into clear, practical guidance for everyday people. Each book builds on the last, taking you from basic understanding to advanced mastery of how to use home equity safely, intelligently, and profitably across every stage of life.

Book 1 — *HELOC Fundamentals*This book gives you the foundation. You will understand how Home Equity Lines of Credit work, how they are structured, how risk is controlled, and how equity becomes usable capital. The books that follow are designed to help you apply that knowledge to your own situation, your income type, your credit profile, and your long-term financial goals.

Book 2 — *How to Qualify for a HELOC* This book shows you how lenders actually evaluate borrowers. You will learn how credit scores, income, property type, and debt ratios affect approval, limits, and interest rates. You will also learn how to position yourself to qualify for the largest possible credit line at the best possible terms.

Book 3 — *HELOCs for Real Estate Investors* This book focuses on using home equity to buy, rehab, refinance, and scale rental properties. It explains how investors use HELOCs for down payments, renovations, and portfolio growth while keeping cash flow positive and risk controlled.

Book 4 — *Self-Employed HELOC Strategies* Designed for business owners, freelancers, 1099 borrowers, and LLCs, this book explains how bank-statement income, business income, and alternative documentation can be used to qualify for home equity even when traditional tax returns do not reflect true cash flow.

Book 5 — *Credit Mastery for HELOC Approval* This book dives deep into credit strategy. You will learn how utilization, credit mix, and reporting behavior affect HELOC limits and pricing—and how to optimize your credit profile specifically for home equity approval.

Book 6 — *No-Doc & Alternative HELOC Programs* This book covers asset-based HELOCs, no-income-verification options, and non-traditional lending programs for high-net-worth, self-employed, or cash-heavy borrowers who do not fit inside standard underwriting models.

Book 7 — *Using a HELOC to Eliminate Debt* This book teaches how to use home equity to replace high-interest credit cards, personal loans, and auto loans with low-interest revolving credit, allowing borrowers to eliminate debt years faster and save tens of thousands of dollars in interest.

Book 8 — *Using a HELOC to Build Wealth* This book shows how homeowners fund investments, businesses, and passive income streams using HELOCs while maintaining liquidity and controlling risk.

Book 9 — *HELOC Risk Management* This book focuses entirely on safety. You will learn how to structure buffers, cash-flow coverage, rate protection, and leverage limits so your home becomes safer over time—not more vulnerable.

Book 10 — *The Smart Borrower's Home Equity Blueprint* The final book ties everything together into a complete lifetime strategy for using home equity as a personal banking system, investment engine, and financial safety net.

Book 11 — *The Cashflow Accelerator Method*

The Cashflow Accelerator Method is the final transformation stage of *The Home Equity Wealth Series.* While the earlier books teach how to access, qualify for, and safely use home equity, this book teaches how to **weaponize cash flow itself** to permanently eliminate debt and create lasting wealth.

Together, these books are designed to turn a single asset—your home—into a lifelong financial advantage. Each volume adds another layer of understanding, allowing you to move from homeowner to capital manager, from borrower to strategist, and from financial stress to long-term stability.

This is not about taking more risk.It is about learning how money really works—and using that knowledge to build financial freedom that lasts.

Educational & Financial Disclaimer

This book is provided for **educational and informational purposes only**. The author and publisher are not engaged in rendering legal, tax, accounting, investment, or financial advice. Although the author is a licensed mortgage broker, the information in this book is intended to provide general education about Home Equity Lines of Credit (HELOCs) and home equity strategy, not personalized financial, legal, or lending advice.

Mortgage programs, underwriting guidelines, interest rates, credit requirements, and home equity products vary by lender, investor, state, and economic conditions, and may change at any time without notice. The examples, calculations, and scenarios presented in this book are hypothetical and are for illustration only. They do not represent guaranteed outcomes or actual loan approvals.

Before making any financial decisions, including applying for a HELOC, refinancing, borrowing against home equity, or using credit for investment or debt repayment, readers should consult with a qualified mortgage professional, financial advisor, tax advisor, or attorney who can evaluate their specific situation.

Risk Disclosure

Borrowing against home equity involves risk. A HELOC is secured by your home, which means failure to make required payments could result in foreclosure or loss of property. This book teaches responsible, conservative, and structured use of home equity, but no financial strategy is risk-free.

Readers are solely responsible for their financial decisions. Neither the author nor the publisher makes any warranties, express or implied, about the accuracy, completeness, or applicability of the information in this book to any individual or situation.

www.ingramcontent.com/pod-product-compliance
Ingram Content Group UK Ltd.
Pitfield, Milton Keynes, MK11 3LW, UK
UKHW020157290926
15471UKWH00005B/915

9 798295 574009